LONDON, NEW YORK, MELBOURNE,
MUNICH, AND DELHI

Editor Niki Foreman
Senior editor Fran Jones
Assistant editor Jenny Finch
Senior art editor Smiljka Surla
Art editors Sheila Collins, Spencer Holbrook,
Philip Letsu, and Stefan Podhorodecki
Managing editor Linda Esposito
Managing art editor Diane Thistlethwaite
Publishing manager Andrew Macintyre
Category publisher Laura Buller
Design development manager Sophia M Tampakopoulos
Picture research Louise Thomas
DK picture library Claire Bowers
Production controller Erica Rosen
DTP designer Andy Hilliard
Jacket editor Mariza O'Keeffe
Jacket designers Jacqui Swan, Smiljka Surla

Illustrations Dave Cockburn

First published in Great Britain in 2007 by
Dorling Kindersley Limited,
80 Strand,
London WC2R 0RL

Copyright © 2007 Dorling Kindersley Limited, London
A Penguin Company

2 4 6 8 10 9 7 5 3 1
FD126 – 12/06

ISBN: 978-1-40531-873-0

Jacket colour reproduction by Colourscan, Singapore
Inside colour reproduction by Wyndeham pre-press, London
Printed and bound by Hung Hing, China

Discover more at
www.dk.com

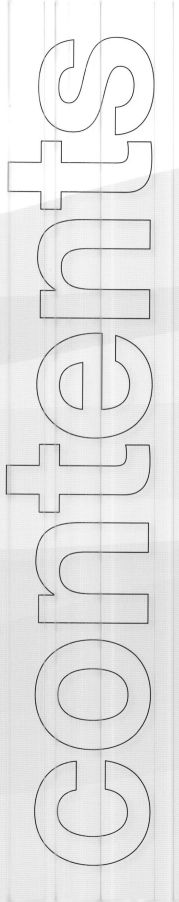

contents

What is energy?

Energy drives our world. We put petrol in our cars, food in our stomachs, and batteries in our toys because everything in our world needs energy to make it happen. Energy makes our world buzz with light, colour, sound, and motion. Without it, life would not be possible – nothing could grow, move, or feel, and the world would be a dark, cold, and lifeless place.

This mobile phone has a **battery** that stores electric power – energy extracted from coal.

The **water** in this bottle originally came from rain clouds, and was driven to Earth by the Sun's energy.

Where did energy first come from?

Most of our energy comes from the Sun, which powers our world like a gigantic battery. But where did the Sun get its energy from? Scientists think that all energy was created at the start of the Universe, in a gigantic explosion called the Big Bang. No more energy has been created since or will ever be made in the future.

Energy is everywhere

Everything is either matter or energy – and matter (the "stuff" all around us, such as the water and trainers seen here) is itself a type of energy. A basic law of the Universe says we cannot create or destroy energy, only change it from one form to another. Everything in the world involves matter or energy changing from one form into another.

Springy trainer soles store and release energy with each step.

In a single second…

…the Sun makes enough power to supply energy to Earth for one million years.

…Earth's population uses as much energy as there is in 3,000 tonnes (tons) of oil.

…more than 750 barrels of oil are pumped out of the ground.

…a single wind turbine generates enough electricity to make 60 cups of tea.

Energy is often invisible

Sometimes we can see energy, such as when the Sun shines or when a fire burns red hot. More often, though, energy is invisible. The blazing summer Sun has made these rocks hot enough to fry an egg, but the rocks look the same as they would on a cold winter's day. The heat is invisible.

Unharnessed energy

Raging oceans, lightning bolts, and blazing sunlight all contain huge amounts of energy. But, although we are surrounded by energy, there is little we have the means to capture and use. A torrential rainstorm, falling over a large area, would release enough potential energy to power a jumbo jet from London to New York.

Muscles convert blood sugar and stored body fat into useful energy.

Recycling energy

Energy is never "used up" – it is constantly recycled into other forms. Trees use energy from sunlight to grow. Although we destroy a tree when we burn it, we don't destroy the energy it contains. When the wood from the tree is burnt, this energy is released as heat and light.

Potential energy

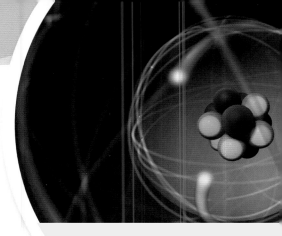

All the energy in our world falls into one of two types. It is either actively doing something, or it is stored, ready to make things happen in the future. Energy that is stored is called potential energy, because it has the ability (or potential) to do something later.

Potential energy can exist in many different forms – in the core of the Sun as well as in the legs of a jumping flea. There are five different categories of potential energy: positional, electrical, nuclear, chemical, and mechanical.

Positional potential energy
A boulder perched on top of a hill has the potential to roll down, gathering speed as it does so. In other words, it has lots of stored potential energy because of its position. In the same way, people on the upper floors of an office block have more potential energy than those lower down, due to their position.

People on the top floor have the most potential energy.

People eight floors up have eight times more potential energy than those on the first floor.

Electrical potential energy
As thunderclouds rumble through the sky, ice crystals and water droplets jostle inside them. This causes electrical energy (static electricity) to build up in the thundercloud, with the potential to release that built-up, stored electrical energy in the form of a lightning bolt. A thundercloud, therefore, has electrical potential energy.

Nuclear potential energy

Everything in the world is made from tiny particles called atoms. Atoms are built from even smaller particles, which are held together by energy. Most of an atom's matter is concentrated in its centre, or nucleus. When an atom splits, its nucleus disintegrates and releases energy. Since an atom can release energy from its nucleus, we say it has nuclear potential energy.

Someone standing up has more potential energy than someone sitting down.

Chemical potential energy

Female glow-worms store two chemicals, called luciferin and luciferase, in their abdomens. When they flash their tails to attract a mate, they convert the potential energy in these chemicals into light. In other words, glow-worms contain a store of chemical potential energy. Batteries also store chemical potential energy.

Mechanical potential energy

When this musician blows air into his cheeks, he stores potential energy that his trumpet can convert into sound energy. Similarly, when a bowstring is pulled back, it has enough stored energy to fire an arrow through the air. These are examples of mechanical (or elastic) potential energy, because they involve a change in shape.

A flea stores energy in its legs, ready to jump…

Using and storing potential energy

It takes effort to walk up stairs because the force of gravity is constantly pulling down on your body. As you climb upwards, you have to work against this force, using energy stored in your body. The higher you climb, the more work you've done to get there and the more energy you've used. At the same time, the more you climb, the more potential energy you have gained. So, when you reach the eighth floor, your body has used energy by climbing, but has gained just as much potential energy getting there.

How is energy measured?	Energy units	Low-energy lamp	Hot cup of coffee	Nuclear power plant
	Energy is measured in units called Joules (J). One Joule is the amount of energy needed to lift a 100 g (3.5 oz) apple 1 m (3 ft) above the ground.	uses	contains	makes
		11 J per second	**34,000 J** of energy	**1,600,000,000 J** per second

Energy of movement

Fleas can leap an incredible 33 cm (13 in) – more than 100 times their own body length. They do this using potential energy stored in their leg muscles. When they jump, their muscles turn the potential energy into kinetic energy, launching them into the air.

Energy in action

Anything that has potential energy can use it to do things. A roller coaster at the top of a hill can use its potential energy to race downwards and pick up speed. The potential energy is gradually used up, but it does not disappear. Instead, it is converted into kinetic energy. Things have kinetic energy when they are moving or doing something. There are five types of kinetic energy: electrical, sound, thermal, light, and the energy of movement.

Converting potential energy

As a roller-coaster car goes down and up hills, it repeatedly converts positional potential energy into moving kinetic energy, and back again. However, some energy is always wasted, working against the forces of air resistance and friction. This is why the car will always lose energy and will, eventually, come to a halt.

Kinetic energy peaks when car races through the dips between hills.

Potential energy peaks at the top of the hills.

Kinetic energy carries the car up the hills, and turns back into potential energy.

Ride ends when most of the potential energy has been lost to friction.

Electrical energy

The electrical potential energy stored in thunderclouds is released as bolts of lightning that strike the ground. Each bolt converts some of the cloud's static electricity (electrical potential energy) into an electric current (electrical kinetic energy). When a lightning bolt strikes the ground, it releases about as much energy as a medium-sized power station generates in one second.

Sound energy

By pulling back the strings of a harp, you give them potential energy. Releasing them converts this potential energy into kinetic energy as the strings vibrate. The vibrating strings shake the air molecules all around them, carrying the sound energy through the air.

Thermal energy

Heat is a kind of kinetic energy – sometimes called thermal energy. When a hob burns gas, it turns the chemical potential energy stored in the gas into heat energy. The heat energy here causes the water molecules in the pan to move about quickly, bringing the water to the boil and cooking the peas.

Light energy

Light is another kind of kinetic energy. It is made from waves of electricity and magnetism moving between two places, along a straight line, carrying energy as they go. This is called electromagnetic radiation (or, sometimes, radiant energy). No other type of energy travels faster than light, which can race seven times around the world in a second.

Hot or cold?

Heat is one of the most important forms of energy in our world. Without the Sun's heat, life on Earth would be impossible. If there were no fire, people would not be able to keep warm or cook food, let alone drive cars or fire rockets into space. Yet cold is important too. Many creatures can only survive in freezing climates, and even people need cold sometimes, such as for preserving foods. However, hot and cold are not clear-cut opposites. An iceberg is exceptionally hot compared to absolute zero – the lowest theoretical temperature – while a summer's day on Earth would seem positively chilly compared to the hot core of the Sun.

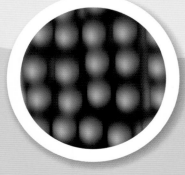

Hot – atoms zoom around

Warm – atoms move quickly

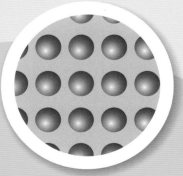

Cold – atoms move slowly

What is heat energy?

If you could see the water molecules inside a hot cup of coffee, they would be zooming around, bouncing off one another like bumper cars. Hot things have heat energy because of the speed at which their atoms or molecules zoom about. In colder objects, atoms or molecules move more slowly, so they have less heat energy.

Absolute zero

Suppose you could cool down an ice cube so much that the molecules inside it stopped moving altogether. At this point the ice would contain no heat energy at all. This temperature is called absolute zero and is equal to -273°C (-470°F). Absolute zero is only a theoretical temperature. So far, this has not been achieved, but scientists have got fairly close – within a few billionths of a degree.

Freezing

Food goes bad because bacteria breed inside it and make it go rotten. On hot summer days, bacteria multiply faster and food goes off more quickly. We freeze food because it slows down the growth of bacteria. The colder you keep something, the longer it will last. We cook food for the same reason – high temperatures kill off harmful bacteria, making food safer to eat.

Wind chill

When the wind blows, it removes heat energy from our bodies more quickly so we cool faster and feel colder. The faster the wind blows, the colder we feel – even if the temperature stays the same. On a winter's day, if the temperature is freezing and a gale is blowing, the temperature will feel about 20 degrees colder and ice will form much faster. This effect is called wind chill.

Red hot

Fires and furnaces give off light as well as heat. When steel is heated to about 1,000°C (1,750°F), it glows red hot. As the atoms inside it absorb heat from the fire, they release energy called electromagnetic radiation. Some of this streams into our eyes as red and yellow light. We can feel the rest of the energy on our skin as a type of "invisible light" called infrared radiation.

Desert heat

One of the hottest places on Earth is Death Valley, California, in the USA, where summer temperatures reach a sizzling 54°C (130°F). The valley is hot because it is deep: parts of it are 86 m (282 ft) below sea level. Its high mountains trap the Sun's heat and funnel it down onto the valley floor. But, at night, when the Sun's energy disappears, the valley quickly becomes very cold.

Rocket exhaust

Almost like magic, the Space Shuttle's main engine makes heat out of cold. Its hydrogen fuel is stored as an icy liquid at -252°C (-423°F), but instantly heats to more than 3,300°C (6,000°F). The Shuttle uses 100 tonnes (tons) of liquid hydrogen in about eight minutes, reaching speeds 70 times faster than a racing car to launch into space.

How is heat measured?

When things heat up, their atoms and molecules move more quickly and their temperature increases. Temperature is a measurement of how fast the atoms are moving. A thermometer, like this liquid-crystal strip, shows something's temperature instantly. Unless we are ill, our bodies are almost always the same temperature, 37°C (98.4°F).

How much heat is in an iceberg?

An iceberg contains more heat energy than a hot cup of coffee. Although the iceberg is colder in temperature, it contains many more water molecules, which still move about with heat energy. Added together, all its chilly, slow-moving ice molecules hold more heat because there are far more of them.

How energy travels

One-way journey

Left undisturbed, hot cups of coffee will always get colder and ice creams will always melt. This is because energy travels from order to chaos – from the calm of the coffee cup to the swirling mist of rising steam above – and never the other way.

Most energy arrives on Earth after a long-distance, but quick, trip from the Sun – 149 million km (93 million miles) in just over eight minutes. This is not the end of its journey though – once it reaches Earth, it travels through our world, changing repeatedly from one form into another, until it finally ends up in the atmosphere as useless "waste heat".

Radiation

When you sit by a fire, you can feel the heat on your face, even if you are some distance away. Heat energy can travel through air – or even, as the Sun proves, through empty space. This process is called radiation. Thanks to radiation, bread cooks quickly in a toaster, even though it does not touch the red-hot wires.

Conduction

One of the ways in which heat energy travels is by conduction. When a hot object, like a fire, touches a colder object, like a pan, energy moves directly from the hot to the cold object. Atoms and molecules in the fire are jiggling around with violent energy. When they touch atoms and molecules in the pan, they jostle into them and pass their energy over.

Elements turn electrical energy into heat energy that cooks the bread.

Convection

When you heat one part of a liquid or gas, it begins to swirl, spreading the heat throughout. This process is called convection. The burner at the bottom of this hot-air balloon heats only the lowest part of the air inside, but convection swirls the warming air upwards and keeps the whole balloon hot.

Wire brings in electrical energy from power supply.

Devastating effects

We may not notice energy as it travels, but we can often feel it and see its effects when it reaches its destination. Earthquakes happen when energy is released by rock movements inside the Earth that shudder outwards in waves. We do not "see" earthquakes until the energy reaches the surface, where it can buckle bridges and topple skyscrapers.

Reflective metal inside toaster concentrates heat on the bread.

Where does energy go?

When two cars collide, their kinetic energy seems to vanish. But there is, in fact, just as much energy after the crash as there was before – it has just been turned into several other forms. Some of the energy makes the car bodies crumple, some makes the sound of the crash, and some ends up as heat. We can never destroy energy, just as we can never create it.

Compressed spring contains potential energy, which converts into kinetic energy to throw the toast upwards.

Heat death

The Sun's energy is vital to life on Earth, but eventually it will all be converted into heat energy that we can no longer use. Some scientists think the Universe itself will end when all the available energy in it has been turned to waste heat. This idea is called heat death.

Releasing energy

When a forest fire blazes, it can destroy in minutes what nature took hundreds of years to create. Fire is one of the most destructive things in our world – but it is also one of the most useful. When people first discovered how to make fire, they found a way to release the energy in fuels, such as wood and coal, providing a way to keep warm and cook food. Today, fire helps us to generate electricity, power car engines and space rockets, and fuel the factories that make important materials such as iron and steel.

The fire triangle
Fires burn when oxygen, fuel, and heat are present. Removing any of these three things stops the chemical reaction. Fire fighters use this idea, called "breaking the fire triangle", to put out fires. Spraying water stops a fire by removing heat, and using foam stops it by removing oxygen. All fires eventually stop when the fuel runs out.

HEAT · OXYGEN · FUEL

Spark provides a tiny input of energy to kick-start combustion.

Oxygen (O_2) from the air reacts with the fuel.

Fuel is made up of carbon, hydrogen, and oxygen atoms.

Water (H_2O) is produced, often as steam.

Carbon dioxide (CO_2) is also produced, and emitted (released) into the atmosphere.

Energy from the fuel is released.

Combustion process
When fire burns, a chemical reaction called combustion takes place. During combustion, the fuel – made mostly from carbon and hydrogen atoms – burns with oxygen from the air. This causes the molecules to break up and release the energy contained within the fuel. As the atoms rearrange themselves, water (as steam) and carbon dioxide are produced and released into the atmosphere.

Strike a match
Items do not catch fire by themselves – they need energy to kick-start things. Striking a match provides a small amount of "activation energy" to start combustion. When you strike a match, friction between the match tip and the box creates a small amount of heat. This causes chemicals on the match tip to catch fire and ignite the wooden stick.

Chemical combustion factory

A candle is a miniature chemical factory that steadily converts the chemical energy stored in wax into light and heat. When you light the wick, heat flows down it by conduction and melts the wax at the top of the candle. The hot wax then makes a vapour that travels up the wick and burns, giving the candle its characteristic wavering flame. The flame gives off energy as heat and light.

Ignition temperatures

Match head
catches fire at
160°C
320°F

Paper
catches fire at
233°C
451°F

Wood
catches fire at
300°C
570°F

Petrol
catches fire at
400°C
750°F

Unburned fuel
Smoke is made in the yellow part of the flame, where there is not enough oxygen to burn the carbon atoms completely. The unburned carbon is released as soot particles that mix with air to make smoke.

Tip of flame
Hot gases funnel up through the inside of the flame, as they do in a chimney, so most heat energy is delivered at the tip. The thin tip is the part of a flame that moves most in a breeze. This causes it to cool slightly and look redder.

Burning carbon particles
Vaporized wax is broken up into atoms of hydrogen and carbon. Hydrogen burns invisibly, but the carbon particles burn in oxygen from the air, giving off heat and light and producing a yellow flame.

Wax vapours drawn into flame
The base of the flame vaporizes the liquid wax. The vaporized wax is a mixture of gases made of hydrogen and carbon. Heat sweeps these gases up from the wick into the higher parts of the flame. Little or no light is produced here.

Complete combustion
There is most oxygen at the base of the flame. This is where the flame burns at its cleanest and hottest – almost invisibly or with a blue hue. Carbon and hydrogen from the wax burn completely to form invisible carbon dioxide gas.

Cord wick
Capillary action (the way liquids rise in thin tubes) draws hot melted wax up the wick to the base of the flame.

Melted wax
Heat from the wick and flame makes a small pool of wax around the top of the candle.

Explosions

It takes hours to release the potential energy locked in a tank of petrol or a lump of coal, but an explosion can free just as much energy in a matter of seconds. Often, an explosion is a process in which two or more chemicals react together to make a huge blast of fast-moving gas. Explosions can be very destructive when they happen in confined spaces. Harnessed properly, however, their energy can be useful or even entertaining.

Stellar explosions

Old stars do not die or fade away. After shining for millions or billions of years, the most massive stars finally run out of energy and collapse in on themselves with a spectacular explosion called a supernova. Unlike explosions on Earth, a supernova can blaze for weeks or months, and leave a cloud of debris that remains for thousands of years.

"Stars" are carefully arranged in each section to make attractive patterns.

"Stars" in second section ignite and begin to explode, releasing more light, sound, and heat.

Burning fuse ignites more "stars" in the upper section.

Second section of firework continues with fuse still burning.

Fireworks

When a firework is lit, the energy from the match kick-starts a series of explosions. At the base of the tube, gunpowder flings the rocket high into the air.

Higher parts of the rocket then explode, turning chemical potential energy into four types of kinetic energy: light, heat, sound, and motion.

"Stars" explode spectacularly in mid-air, converting stored chemical energy into light, sound, and heat.

Fuse runs through the entire length of the firework.

Fuse burns slowly upwards, setting off explosive "stars" in the bottom section.

Lit fuse ignites the gunpowder at the base of the firework.

Life-saving explosion

When a car crashes, an electrical sensor detects the impact and triggers the air bags. Inside each air bag, two chemicals, called sodium azide and potassium nitrate, react together explosively. The explosion generates a huge cloud of nitrogen gas moving at 320 km/h (200 mph). Air bags save lives because they inflate quickly enough to cushion the passengers from the impact of the crash.

Champagne corks

Explosions can happen without fire, and sometimes even without heat. Champagne contains a trapped gas called carbon dioxide. When you loosen the cork, the gas is released and the cork flies out with a pop – a mini explosion.

Explosive demolition

When a stick of dynamite explodes, it produces a huge volume of gas that moves 10 times faster than a military jet. Such a blast instantly weakens a building's structure, leaving gravity to pull the pieces to the ground. As the building tumbles, its huge potential energy turns into kinetic energy, heat, and a rumbling boom of sound.

About 80 per cent of the energy people use comes from coal, oil, and gas. We use these "fossil fuels" in enormous quantities for good reasons. They are easy to store and move, and the energy in them can be quickly released for cooking, heating, and transportation. Unfortunately, we are now using fossil fuels at an alarming rate. Some were formed before dinosaurs walked on Earth, but most will be gone by the end of this century.

Coal supplies 24 per cent of world energy

Oil supplies 35 per cent of world energy

Gas supplies 21 per cent of world energy

Derrick (drilling tower) supports the weight of the drill string.

Fossil fuels

Three types of fossil fuels

Coal became the world's number one fuel after steam engines were invented in the 18th century. Though less popular today, it is still used to make electricity in power stations. In the mid-19th century, oil use grew rapidly following the invention of the petrol engine. Gas, the cleanest fossil fuel, has been used for heating and cooking since the early 20th century.

How fossil fuels are formed

Fossil fuels are made from animals and plants that died millions of years ago. Bacteria break down their remains, which are squeezed beneath layers of rock and slowly cooked by Earth's heat. Oil and gas form mostly under the sea – oil where the temperature is lower, gas where it is hotter. Coal is made from buried and compressed land plants.

Plant matter (dead plants)	Peat (rotting plants)	Lignite (brown coal)	Bituminous coal (low-quality coal)	Anthracite (high-quality coal)
360 million years ago ➝		90 million years ago ➝		Today ➝

Motor in the derrick rotates the drill string, which can be more than 10 km (6 miles) long.

Buildings house the drilling crew and control rooms.

Cranes haul the drill sections and equipment into position.

How fuel is extracted

Offshore rigs extract oil using a long, deep "drill string" joined together from hundreds of 9-m (30-ft) pipes. With a diamond bit (cutting blade) mounted on the end, the drill string bores down through several kilometres (miles) of rock until it reaches the oil. Oil forms under pressure, which causes it to squirt back up the hole to be piped or shipped ashore.

Legs support rig up to 100 m (328 ft) above seabed.

Petroleum products

The petrol we use in our cars is made from petroleum ("crude oil") drilled from the ground. Before we can use petroleum, it has to be refined. Refining separates petroleum into many chemicals, all based on hydrogen and carbon. Some become oils of different kinds, while others make plastics. A plastic toothbrush or rubber duck in your bathroom might be made from petroleum that started off 20 million years ago in the body of a seahorse!

When will fossil fuels run out?	Oil	Gas	Coal
	by the year	by the year	by the year
	2050	2100	2250

Engine power

Whether you are travelling to school or to the Moon, engines get you there quickly and efficiently. Engines are amongst the world's most important inventions. An engine is a machine that burns or explodes a fuel in a carefully controlled process that releases heat. The heat is then converted into kinetic energy to power a vehicle along. Just over a quarter of all the energy people use goes to fuel engines – transport is the world's second biggest user of energy, after industry.

Petrol-powered boat

This boat's outboard motor is a simple engine, which burns petrol to drive the boat through the water. The large black petrol tank on top feeds fuel to a cylinder underneath. Inside the cylinder, the petrol mixes with oxygen from the air. This is then ignited by a "spark plug" to release heat energy in a mini explosion, driving a "piston" that makes the boat's propeller spin. This process happens over and over to generate the boat's power.

Coal-powered train

This steam engine is like a coal-powered kettle with wheels. The long cylinder at the front contains a water boiler, heated by a coal-powered furnace where the coal burns and releases its energy as heat. The heat turns the water in the boiler to steam, which pushes pistons back and forth to turn the wheels.

Hydrogen-powered rocket engine

Rocket engines must produce huge amounts of power to launch from Earth into space. In space, there is no air, and so rockets have an oxygen tank, as well as a fuel tank, to enable combustion to take place. Rocket engines burn a variety of fuels – some use a type of kerosene called RP-1 (Refined Petroleum-1), and others use liquid hydrogen, which releases power more quickly.

Kerosene-powered jet engine

A jet plane weighs 100 times more than a car, and must go 10 times faster to stay in the air. Therefore, its engines must make more power much more quickly than a car engine does. A jet engine does just that, by sucking in air at the front to burn with fuel and release heat. This energy is then used to blast hot air out of the back, thrusting the plane forwards.

Nitromethane-powered drag car

Drag cars are racing cars powered by jets or modified petrol engines. Most "dragsters" burn an energy-rich fuel called nitromethane, which makes power three times more quickly than petrol. They go so fast that they are unable to take corners and so only race in straight lines – the race usually ending after a quarter of a mile.

Diesel train

Diesel engines, used in many modes of transport, are similar to petrol engines. Like petrol, diesel is a type of refined oil that is burned in the engine. Instead of using a spark plug, the diesel engine ignites its fuel by compressing it more intensely. This causes it to explode by itself under the pressure, making diesel engines more efficient.

Powerful engines

Typical speeds that each engine can reach for each mode of transport

Outboard motor	80 km/h (50 mph)
Steam engine	120 km/h (75 mph)
Diesel locomotive	160 km/h (100 mph)
Drag-car engine	530 km/h (330 mph)
Jet engine	900 km/h (550 mph)
Rocket engine	40,500 km/h (25,100 mph)

Food as fuel

The heart beats more than 200 times a minute, pumping energy around the body in blood.

From cycling and smiling to thinking and sleeping, everything you do uses energy. Just like the engine in a car, your body uses fuel and oxygen to make its energy –but there are no pistons and cylinders inside you. Your stomach turns the food you eat into a simple type of sugar called glucose. Your blood carries the glucose around your body, mixed with oxygen from your lungs. When you move, your muscles use the glucose and oxygen to make the energy they need.

A boiled, peeled potato contains 117 calories (489 kJ) of energy – enough to boil the water for 14 cups of tea.

A stick of celery contains 6 calories (27 kJ) of energy, using more to digest than it actually supplies.

5 medium bananas contain 525 calories (2205 kJ) of energy – enough for an hour's vigorous swimming.

150 pasta twists contain 209 calories (873 kJ) of energy – enough for an hour's moderate walking.

A slice of bread contains 65 calories (270 kJ) of energy – enough to power a 60-watt lamp for 1 hour 30 minutes.

2 chocolate biscuits contain 280 calories (400 kJ) of energy – enough to allow you to run for 40 minutes.

70 g (2.5 oz) of beans contain 20 calories (84 kJ) of energy – enough to supply a mouse's energy needs for one day.

2 slices of steak contain 360 calories (1,500 kJ) of energy – enough to power a small car for 10 seconds.

A large boiled egg contains 156 calories (648 kJ) of energy – enough to play table tennis for an hour.

Leg muscles convert the body's chemical potential energy into kinetic (movement) energy.

Bicycle helps the body to use its energy more efficiently, going further faster.

Energy from food

Food stores potential energy in chemical form. The amount of energy we can get by eating a particular food is measured in calories or kilojoules (kJ). Different types of food have more or fewer calories because they store more or less energy. With this information, we can ensure we eat a balanced diet to provide us with the energy we need to function and move.

How the body uses energy

Your body makes energy in different ways. For a sudden burst of high energy, it uses a type of glucose stored in its muscles and liver. It can do this for only 15–30 minutes, however, before the energy store runs out. For longer, less intense exercise, our bodies burn stored body fat.

Brain cells are constantly active. Each brain cell uses twice the amount of energy as other body cells.

Eyes take in microscopic amounts of light energy.

Arm muscles make energy from glucose and fat.

Lungs take in oxygen, which is needed to convert glucose into energy.

Carnivore

Carnivore (meat-eater)

Herbivore (plant-eater)

Plants

Energy pyramid

Food chains work in a pyramid shape with many plants at the bottom and just a few carnivores at the top. This is because the further up the food chain you go, the less food (and hence energy) remains available. A food chain cannot have more than four or five links, because there would not be enough food for the animals at the top of the chain.

Storing food

Gila monsters, which live in deserts in the USA, can go for months without eating. After a hearty meal of a rat, mouse, frog, or bird, they store energy as fat in their long thick tails. When food supplies are scarce, they live off this store, turning the fat back into energy again.

Light energy

Energy leaves the Sun in the form of light and heat.

Plants capture the energy and store it as chemical potential energy.

Chemical energy

Food contains chemical energy made by plants.

Your body stores the chemical energy from food as fat and other substances.

Kinetic energy

Muscles turn potential chemical energy into kinetic energy when you move.

Converting energy

Your bicycle and your body are both solar powered. The energy they use has been transformed several times since it first started out from the Sun. The energy that helps you to cycle today may have started as a sunbeam three or four years ago.

Daily intake of calories

Hummingbird	Cat	Human	Elephant
A hummingbird consumes about	A cat consumes about	A human consumes about	An elephant consumes about
10	**300**	**2,500**	**40,000**
calories per day	calories per day	calories per day	calories per day

Wasting energy

Hair traps heat inside head.

Skin is designed to cool the body through perspiration, so heat loss here is high.

Clothes help to retain heat, with layers trapping air and providing better insulation.

Extremities like fingers and toes are colder than the rest of the body.

We can measure how much energy is wasted by comparing the amount of useful work something does with the amount of energy in its fuel. A bicycle is extremely efficient because it turns about 90 per cent of the energy your body supplies, through pedalling, into useful kinetic energy. Our homes, cars, and cities are much less efficient. Cars waste 75–80 per cent of the fuel they use in generating unnecessary heat and noise. Unless buildings are very well insulated, their heat gradually escapes through the roof, windows, and walls. A typical home wastes 50 per cent of the energy supplied to it.

Inefficient body

Your body is only about 25 per cent efficient. In other words, for every 10 meals you eat, your body wastes the energy from seven and a half of them. A lot of this wasted energy is lost as heat, which is why wearing clothes to stop heat escaping in cold weather is so important. This thermogram, taken with a heat-sensitive camera, shows which parts of the body waste the most energy.

City waste

An old-fashioned light bulb wastes around 90 per cent of the electricity it uses by getting hot. A modern, energy-saving light bulb uses 80 per cent less energy and lasts 10 times longer. Installing three energy-saving lights in every home would save enough energy to power all the world's streetlights.

Waste power

Power stations use river or sea water to cool down their machinery, wasting a huge amount of heat energy in cooling towers like these. Even more energy is wasted transmitting electricity to the point of use. In fact, two thirds of the fuel supplied to a power station is wasted before the energy it generates reaches our homes.

Wasting resources

Gas is sometimes found in oil reserves, which can be dangerous as it has the potential to explode. To overcome this problem, the gas is burnt off in chimneys called flares. The gas wasted in flares each year would be enough to supply the entire world for 20 days.

Friction – useful or wasteful?

Friction is the force at work when two things rub together, and it can be very helpful. The friction between tyres and tarmac keeps a car on the road when it goes round a corner. However, friction also wastes a great deal of energy. When a car travelling at 50 km/h (30 mph) stops quickly, its brakes generate enough heat through friction to make several cups of tea.

BMW Power

Energy day

Everything we do each day uses a certain amount of energy. Energy is a bit like money, which we need to save up before we can spend it to do things. Every day we have to balance the budget by saving enough energy to fund our active lives. That means fuelling our bodies with enough food and remembering to charge up our mobile phones. Sometimes we are very aware of using energy – after swimming or running, we might feel hungry because our energy is running low. Most of the time, though, we use energy without even thinking about it.

Lunchtime

Eating tops up your energy supply, but it uses energy too. Your jaw muscles use energy when they chew and, once food is in your stomach, you use energy to digest it. That means some of the energy in every meal is always used up turning the food into energy – when you eat lunch for 15 minutes, you use about 85 kJ of energy.

Making breakfast

Breakfast is an important meal because it replenishes the energy your body uses at night. If you eat a cooked breakfast, your body absorbs both the energy in the food and the heat it contains. It takes about 300 kJ of electrical energy to toast six slices of bread.

Walking to school

Loaded up with energy, your body can now embark on the morning's walk. Walking is a cheap and efficient way to travel and keeps your body fit and healthy. Walking briskly for 15 minutes also uses about 300 kJ of energy.

Taking a trip

Car journeys are often quick and easy, but waste huge amounts of energy, especially if only one person is in the car. An average car weighs about 20 times more than its driver, and so requires at least 20 times more energy just to move it, let alone reach top speeds. A typical 10-minute car trip uses about 50,000 kJ of energy – much more than your body uses, even in a highly active day.

Exercising the brain

Your brain uses up to one fifth of your body's total energy supply. It takes its fuel – glucose – from the blood vessels that run through it. Brain cells need twice as much energy as other body cells because they are active all the time in everything you do. Even your thoughts are powered by energy! Studying at a desk, for example, for an hour's lesson requires a surge of brain power using about 85 kJ of energy.

Energetic exercise

Swimming builds your body's stamina, strength, and flexibility. It is an excellent form of aerobic exercise in which your body uses oxygen to burn fats and glucose and release energy. Swimming for an hour uses about 1,200 kJ of energy.

Docile exercise

Sleeping is a form of exercise too. Your muscles may be at rest, but your brain, heart, lungs, and other internal organs are all working the night shift, keeping your body alive. During eight hours of sleep, your body uses the same amount of energy as it does during an hour's swim.

Coping with extremes

From the sizzling deserts to the freezing cold poles, Earth is a place of extremes. The Sun is a vital source of energy, giving life to plants and animals, but different parts of the planet receive different amounts of solar energy. There is always more energy at the Equator than there is at the poles, and all places receive more energy in summer than they do in winter. Sometimes there is too much energy and sometimes too little, so plants and animals have developed clever ways of coping.

In December, the southern hemisphere faces the Sun and receives more heat. It experiences summer.

In March, both hemispheres are heated equally. The northern hemisphere experiences spring, and the southern, autumn.

In September, both hemispheres are heated equally. The northern hemisphere experiences autumn, and the southern, spring.

In June, the northern hemisphere is heated the most and experiences summer. The southern hemisphere experiences winter.

Hot and cold

Earth is curved and spins on a tilt, so the tropics (near the Equator) always receive more solar energy than the poles. Sunlight also has to cut through more atmosphere to reach the poles, and ice and snow reflect 85 per cent of it straight back.

Seeking sunlight

Sunflowers can grow to be as big as dinner plates by absorbing the maximum amount of solar energy possible. As buds, they track the Sun through the sky each day, facing east at dawn and west at dusk.

Huddling together

Very little of the Sun's energy reaches Antarctica. These emperor penguin chicks huddle together to save energy so that they can survive temperatures as low as -60°C (-76°F) and winds of 180 km/h (110 mph).

Sleeping through

In winter, there is less solar energy, fewer plants, and therefore less fuel for animals. Creatures like this dormouse survive by hibernating. During autumn, it eats enough berries and seeds to double its body weight. This energy store keeps it alive during a seven-month sleep. Its heartbeat and breathing slow down, and its body temperature falls to save energy.

Keeping cool

Desert plants, like these agaves, use huge amounts of energy growing flowers up to 12 m (40 ft) tall. The biggest challenge they face is sweltering desert temperatures. They can survive droughts by storing water in thick fleshy leaves. These have a special coating that reflect back incoming heat to reduce the amount of water lost through evaporation.

Avoiding the heat

A good way to survive the desert heat is to sleep in the daytime and feed at night. One of the world's smallest owls, the tiny elf owl, hides until dusk in holes that woodpeckers have drilled into cactus plants. With the day's heat dying down, the owl emerges for a midnight snack of scorpions, moths, and other nocturnal insects.

Storage tanks

Food and water can be in short supply in deserts. Camels ensure that they have plenty by storing fat in their humps, which they turn into energy and water as necessary. When they find a water supply, they can drink five buckets' worth in just 10 minutes. Their thick coats reflect sunlight, and their noses are designed to recycle the moisture that most mammals lose when they breathe out.

The Sun

Behind the calm face of the Sun there lies a stormy secret. Deep inside this hot ball of gas, billions of atoms are smashing together, releasing energy that bubbles up to the surface and fires out through space. This violent process makes the Sun the brightest star that we can see. Producing energy like a giant celestial power station, the Sun then blasts its energy in all directions. There is enough fuel packed inside the Sun's core for it to last another five billion years.

High-energy Sun

The Sun is an energy factory inside a dense ball of gas 100 times wider than Earth. Energy made in the core travels through the Sun's radiative zone by radiation. For the rest of its journey, it travels by convection through the convective zone to the Sun's surface, or photosphere. The sunlight we see comes from the photosphere.

The nuclear furnace

Seen through an X-ray telescope, the Sun bubbles with fire and fury. But it does not make energy by burning fuel. The Sun consists almost entirely of two gases, hydrogen and helium, and works by nuclear power. When atoms of hydrogen smash together, they make helium and release energy in a process called nuclear fusion. Each second, the Sun's core generates as much energy as 100 billion nuclear explosions.

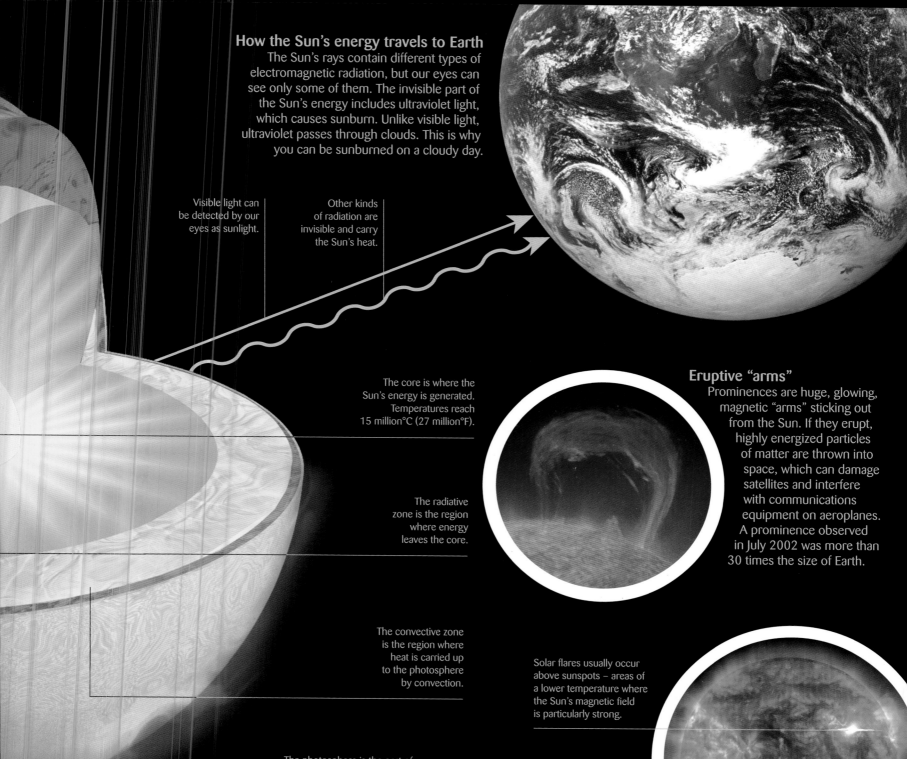

How the Sun's energy travels to Earth

The Sun's rays contain different types of electromagnetic radiation, but our eyes can see only some of them. The invisible part of the Sun's energy includes ultraviolet light, which causes sunburn. Unlike visible light, ultraviolet passes through clouds. This is why you can be sunburned on a cloudy day.

Visible light can be detected by our eyes as sunlight.

Other kinds of radiation are invisible and carry the Sun's heat.

The core is where the Sun's energy is generated. Temperatures reach 15 million°C (27 million°F).

The radiative zone is the region where energy leaves the core.

The convective zone is the region where heat is carried up to the photosphere by convection.

The photosphere is the part of the Sun that emits heat and light. Its temperature is only about 6,000°C (11,000°F).

Eruptive "arms"

Prominences are huge, glowing, magnetic "arms" sticking out from the Sun. If they erupt, highly energized particles of matter are thrown into space, which can damage satellites and interfere with communications equipment on aeroplanes. A prominence observed in July 2002 was more than 30 times the size of Earth.

Solar flares usually occur above sunspots – areas of a lower temperature where the Sun's magnetic field is particularly strong.

Solar flares

The brightest features on the Sun are called solar flares, which usually occur above sunspots. In these magnetic explosions, the Sun emits a massive burst of electromagnetic radiation, including radio waves and light.

Nuclear energy

Atoms are tiny bits of matter that everything in the world is made from. Atoms are built from even smaller particles, which are locked together by energy in the nucleus. Large atoms can release this "nuclear energy" by splitting apart (nuclear fission), while small atoms can release it by joining together (nuclear fusion). Although each atom contains only a tiny amount of energy, trillions together can generate huge amounts of power.

Digging for fuel
The fuel used in nuclear power stations comes from a heavy chemical element called uranium. This is mined as an ore (raw mineral) called uraninite from gigantic pits, like this one in Australia.

Uraninite is a uranium-rich mineral found in the ground.

Nuclear fuel pellets
Uranium ore is ground up and treated chemically to extract the uranium, which is then stored as a dry powder called yellowcake. This is "enriched" to increase its uranium content, and is packaged into either large fuel rods or small pellets, like these. Each pellet contains as much energy as one tonne (ton) of coal.

Nuclear fission

Nuclear power stations and nuclear bombs make energy by splitting atoms, with each splitting atom causing others to split after it in a "chain reaction". In a nuclear bomb, this chain reaction is uncontrolled, producing a huge, devastating explosion and the unmistakable mushroom cloud of smoke and gases.

How nuclear power works

A nuclear power station unlocks the energy in a uranium rod or pellet and turns it into electricity. Inside the dome-shaped reactor, uranium atoms split and give off heat, which is used to make steam. The steam is then pumped to a separate building where it drives a turbine to generate electricity.

Control rods are raised or lowered to speed up or slow down the chain reaction.

Reactor holds fuel rods and allows atoms to split apart safely, generating heat energy.

Thick concrete shield stops radiation escaping in an accident.

Pipe carries steam to separate turbine building.

Generators, powered by the spinning turbine, produce electricity.

Steam flows through the turbine, making it spin like a propeller.

Pylons carry electricity to homes and factories.

Hot water from the reactor boils water in the tank to make steam.

Water cools after leaving the turbine and is piped back for reuse.

Nuclear accidents

Nuclear power stations are usually safe, but, when they go wrong, dangerous amounts of radiation can escape. The world's worst nuclear accident happened in April 1986, when the Chernobyl nuclear power station exploded in the Ukraine. The explosion hurled 100 times more radiation into the air than the atom bombs dropped on Japan in World War II. Westerly winds spread this "fallout" cloud (shown in pink) across Europe.

The future for nuclear energy

The Sun makes energy by a safer kind of nuclear reaction called fusion, where small atoms join together to make bigger ones. In order to make energy this way on Earth, the same conditions as those in the Sun need to be recreated – and this experimental tokamak machine does just that. Like a giant pressure cooker, it heats and squeezes atoms so that they release their energy as they fuse together into a hot soup called a plasma.

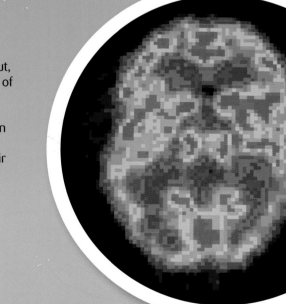

Medicine and research

Nuclear technology plays a crucial role in medical research. In a PET scan, a person's brain is injected with radioactive liquid. As the liquid is absorbed, active parts of the brain (yellow and red) give off more radiation than less active areas (purple and blue). In this image, a computer has mapped these areas to show a sleeping person's brain activity.

Solar energy

Fossil fuels are dwindling, so our energy future lies elsewhere – with renewable forms of power that will never run out. Renewables include solar and geothermal energy, wind and wave power, and biopower. Except for geothermal, they all get their energy from the Sun – so most renewables are actually indirect forms of solar energy. The two most familiar kinds of solar energy involve directly harnessing the Sun's heat to warm water (called solar thermal) and its light to make electricity (called solar electric).

Sunlight on Earth

A huge amount of solar energy reaches Earth. If we could cover just one per cent of the Sahara with solar panels, we could make more than enough electricity to supply the entire world. However, this would only work during daylight.

Solar-electric panels

These "photovoltaic" panels generate electricity from sunlight using an array (grid pattern) of 36 separate cells. Each panel makes enough energy to light a 40-watt lamp. Panels like this are designed to trickle electricity into batteries or the power grid.

Sunlight

1. Inner layer of cell catches the Sun's energy, causing the electrons to jump up to the top layer.

2. Electrons trickle out of the panel into the outside circuit, carrying electrical energy.

Electron

4. Electrons pass back to the bottom layer, completing the circuit.

3. Electrons flow through the lamp, which converts electrical energy into light and heat.

Solar-thermal panels

These solar panels do not make electricity. Instead, they act as part of the building's hot water system. Rather than using the Sun's light, the dark glass sheets trap its heat to warm a grid of water pipes inside them. The hot water is then piped into the building below.

How a solar-electric cell works

"Photovoltaic" means turning light into electricity. Each of the photovoltaic cells in a solar panel is made from a sandwich of different layers. These trap the energy from the Sun's rays and pass it to electrons in the inner layer, which flow out of the panel, carrying electrical energy as they go to power electrical devices.

On the move

This 100-seat passenger boat makes its own power using huge, folding panels. On stormy days, they stand upright and catch the wind like sails. On sunny days, the sails fold down to reveal solar panels, which make enough electricity to power the boat's engine.

Developing countries

Almost a third of the world's people do not have electricity, because many developing countries cannot afford large power stations and transmission lines. Solar power could change all that. A single photovoltaic panel can make enough electricity to light this small reed house in Peru. Solar panels like this are also being used to power telephones and street lights in developing nations.

Wind and water

The Sun is the engine that powers our weather system. It warms Earth unevenly, causing stormy winds that build up waves on the oceans, and it drives the weather that moves water between Earth's surface and its atmosphere. People have been harnessing this kind of energy since windmills and water wheels were first used in ancient times. With fossil fuel supplies running out, wind and water power are becoming important once more – and as renewable energy sources, they will never run out.

Wind generator
Machines called turbines capture the kinetic energy from moving wind or water, and turn it into electricity. A typical wind turbine like this one makes two megawatts of power – enough to supply around 1,000 homes.

Blades are 35 m (115 ft) across and 85 m (280 ft) off the ground.

Generator, connected to the turbine's spinning blades, makes electricity.

Wind power
San Gorgiono Pass in California, USA, is the perfect location for this farm of 3,500 wind turbines. It is a wide, empty channel between two mountain ranges with strong winds that howl through it for much of the year.

Ocean power
A breaking wave
holds enough energy to
power thousands of light bulbs.
Waves carry kinetic energy across
the surface of the oceans, which is
released when they crash on the shore.
Some of this energy can be harnessed to
make electricity. However, the oceans can be
stormy and violent, and wave power machines have
often been destroyed by the very energy they were
designed to capture.

Tidal power
Gravity, mostly from the Moon, pulls
ocean tides up and down beaches and
in and out of estuaries (places where
rivers meet the sea). This bridge-like
barrage spans the Rance river estuary
in northern France. Electricity is made
as the tidal water moves back and forth
through the turbines inside the barrage.

Hydroelectric power
On the Colorado River in the
USA, the Hoover Dam produces
the power for 1.3 million people in
three US states – Nevada, Arizona,
and California. Hydroelectric dams
like this block rivers to create huge
reservoirs. As the water from
the reservoir falls through the dam
to the river in front, its potential
energy turns to kinetic energy.
The water rushes past turbines
that use its kinetic energy
to generate electricity.

Electrical energy

What do all fuels – from fossil fuels and solar, to nuclear and biopower – have in common? They can all be turned into electricity. Electricity is our most useful kind of energy. We can quickly and easily move it from place to place through power lines, and turn it back into almost any other kind of energy, including light, motion, sound, and heat.

Static electricity is potential energy

If you rub a plastic comb on your jumper, you can use it to pick up scraps of paper. The energy you have to use rubbing the comb, working against the friction provided by your jumper, quickly turns into static electricity – electrical potential energy stored in the comb.

NO CURRENT IN AN UNPLUGGED CABLE

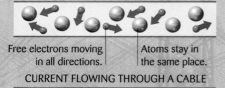

Free electrons moving in all directions. | Atoms stay in the same place.

CURRENT FLOWING THROUGH A CABLE

Free electrons move in the same direction. | Atoms stay in the same place, allowing the current to pass around them.

Electric current is kinetic energy

Simply flicking a switch allows an electric current to flow into your home, through cables, from a power station. Electrical cables are made from metals such as copper, through which electrons can flow freely. When the power is switched on, the electrons march in the same direction, carrying energy like ants carry leaves. An electric current is a kind of kinetic energy because the electrons are constantly moving.

Power grid pylons

Cables carry electrical energy from the power station where it is made to the homes, offices, and factories where it is used. In rural areas, cables run between tall masts called pylons. Every length of cable the electricity travels down wastes a bit of energy. Transmitting electricity at extremely high voltages helps to reduce the amount of energy that is lost.

Electricity into light

Making light was the first thing people learned to do with electricity. Thomas Edison (1847–1931), the US inventor who pioneered electric power, demonstrated a practical light bulb in 1879. It used a thin wire filament, which glowed when electricity flowed through it and made it hot. Four years later, Edison set up the USA's first power station in New York. Towns and cities have blazed with electric light ever since.

Electricity into motion

This toy car contains a battery-powered electric motor connected to the wheels. When you switch on the power, electrical energy flows in a current from the battery to the motor. The motor then converts this electrical energy into motion, turning the wheels to drive the car.

Electricity into sound

Electric guitars are louder than acoustic ones because they use electrical energy to amplify (increase) the noise they make. When the metal strings are plucked, a small electric current is generated. This flows through a cable into an amplifier unit, which uses electricity to boost the signal. The amplified current powers the loudspeakers to make the guitar sound louder.

Electricity into heat

When electrons flow in a current through wires, they have to work against "resistance", which tries to stop them. If there is enough resistance, the wire heats up. Resistance is used by cooker hobs to turn electrical energy into heat.

Making electricity

You can't power a coffee maker with coal, a vacuum cleaner with gas, or a computer with oil. But you can use all these appliances if the coal, gas, or oil are first converted into electricity. Electricity is rapidly becoming the world's favourite energy source, and most of it is made from fossil fuels. One large power station can make enough electricity to supply more than a million homes.

Cooling water

Water can hold more heat than almost any other substance. In centrally heated homes, a loop of water pipes carries heat from the boiler around the house and back again. Similarly, in power stations, water moves heat from the furnace to the turbines, which drive generators to make electricity. The water is then cooled in giant towers and piped back for reuse.

From coal to coffee

Most power stations run on oil, gas, or coal, though other fuels (from uranium to chicken manure) can be used instead. The fuel releases heat, which boils water to create steam. This then drives a generator, and makes electricity.

Power from gas

Gas is the "cleanest" of the fossil fuels. When burned in a power station, it produces much less pollution and less than half the carbon dioxide emissions of a coal-fired station.

Power from oil

Oil-fired power stations burn heavy fuel-oil, and are often built close to petroleum refineries. A large oil-fired power station can make enough electricity to supply two million people.

Power from coal

Coal makes about 40 per cent of the world's electricity – more than any other fuel. Almost half the world's coal-fired power stations are in just two countries: the USA and China.

Chimney gives off waste gases, made in the furnace.

Steam turns the blades inside the turbine.

Fuel – either coal, gas, or oil here – is piped to the furnace.

Furnace burns the fuel to release heat energy.

Water is boiled by the heat from the furnace to make steam.

Power cuts

Electricity is so reliable that we only notice it when it stops working. Most power cuts happen after storms or severe weather. In 1998, an ice storm in North America left more than three million people without electricity. Ten people were killed, flights and trains were cancelled, and many homes were without power for days.

Generator contains magnets and coils of wire, which are spun by the turbine to make electricity.

Electricity flows from the power station at a high voltage to save power.

Substation reduces the voltage to make electricity safe for use in the home.

Steam cools and condenses into hot water.

Cooling tower cools the hot water for reuse.

In the home

Electricity is usually there when we need it. Utility companies know people will use most power at meal-times and in the evenings, and more in winter than in summer. This information helps them to regulate the energy they produce, turning power stations up and down to match demand.

Canada produces 52% more than it uses.

Producers and consumers

On this world map, the coloured-in areas show how much energy certain countries or continents make. The outlined areas show how much energy they use. Where coloured areas spill over the outlines, those countries make more energy than they use. Where the coloured areas are inside the outlines, the countries use more energy than they make.

The USA, including Alaska, uses a third more than it produces.

The UK produces 11% more than it uses.

France uses twice as much as it produces.

In total, Europe uses 16% more than it produces.

Oil pipeline

Oil and gas are transported across land in pipelines like this one, which snakes 1,300 km (800 miles) over Alaska. On its journey, it crosses three mountain ranges and more than 800 rivers and streams. Half the pipeline is on stilts to stop the hot oil inside melting the frozen ground beneath.

South America produces 42% more than it uses.

Energy in our world

The world is an energy-hungry place. However, supplies of oil, gas, and coal are not evenly distributed, which means that some countries produce more than they need, while others need more than they can produce. Energy-rich countries sell their fossil fuels to energy-poor ones, with pipelines and ships carrying oil, gas, and coal to wherever they are needed. Renewable energy, such as wind and hydroelectric power, enables some countries to produce more of their own energy.

Coal mining

Some of the world's biggest coal mines are in Wyoming in the USA. Ten huge pits produce almost 40 per cent of the USA's coal – a fuel that makes half the country's electricity. These giant mines use the world's biggest trucks, each with the capacity to carry more than 400 tonnes (tons) of coal. The world's largest producers of coal are China, followed by the USA and India.

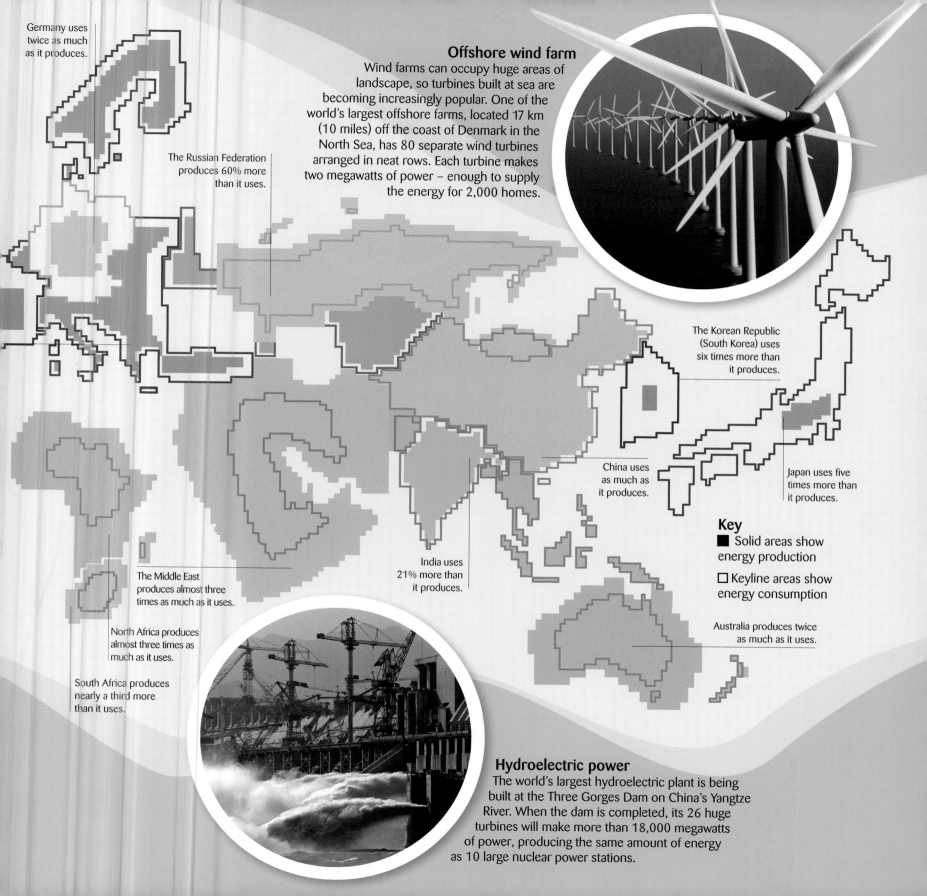

Germany uses twice as much as it produces.

The Russian Federation produces 60% more than it uses.

Offshore wind farm
Wind farms can occupy huge areas of landscape, so turbines built at sea are becoming increasingly popular. One of the world's largest offshore farms, located 17 km (10 miles) off the coast of Denmark in the North Sea, has 80 separate wind turbines arranged in neat rows. Each turbine makes two megawatts of power – enough to supply the energy for 2,000 homes.

The Korean Republic (South Korea) uses six times more than it produces.

China uses as much as it produces.

Japan uses five times more than it produces.

Key
■ Solid areas show energy production

□ Keyline areas show energy consumption

The Middle East produces almost three times as much as it uses.

India uses 21% more than it produces.

Australia produces twice as much as it uses.

North Africa produces almost three times as much as it uses.

South Africa produces nearly a third more than it uses.

Hydroelectric power
The world's largest hydroelectric plant is being built at the Three Gorges Dam on China's Yangtze River. When the dam is completed, its 26 huge turbines will make more than 18,000 megawatts of power, producing the same amount of energy as 10 large nuclear power stations.

Beneath your feet

Packed with pipes and buzzing with energy, there's another world beneath your feet. More than three-quarters of people in developed countries live in towns and cities, where most of the world's energy is used. Urban areas are busy and crowded, so energy has to travel underground to where it is needed. The deepest pipes can be up to 300 m (1,000 ft) below street level.

Street level

City streets hum with energy and life. Cars zoom about converting fuel into heat, sound, and motion. People mill around in all directions, turning food into kinetic energy as they go. TV and radio programmes zap invisibly through the air, as do phone calls. Such random movements of energy are a far cry from the managed system beneath your feet.

Energy paths

Underground, energy follows more systematic paths along a dense network of pipes and cables. Power lines and telecommunications cables run near the surface, with water pipes slightly deeper, and transport pipes deeper still.

Water is pulled along pipes by gravity or pushed along by pressure.

Coaxial cables (wires inside wires) carry cable TV programmes.

Fibre-optic cables can carry millions of phone and Internet calls as pulses of light.

Gas flows through pipes because it is under pressure.

Power cables are heavily insulated (wrapped in plastic) for safety.

Pipes underground

Pipes must be tough to survive decades underground. Early wooden pipes were replaced by cast iron, a material that is prone to rusting and leaking. Today, new pipes are made from plastic, concrete, or steel. Pipes range in diameter from about 2 cm (¾ in) to 6 m (20 ft) – small enough for a worm or large enough for a giraffe!

Old wooden pipes, no longer in use, may still be in place.

Fibre-optic cable

Telephone, cable TV, and Internet signals travel under your feet as flickering pulses of light in fibre-optic cables. Light travels faster than any other kind of energy – up to 300,000 km/s (186,000 miles/s) – which is why it is perfect for communication as there is little delay between sending and receiving the signal.

Tunnelling moles

Tunnel Boring Machines (TBMs), or "moles", are used to dig the biggest pipes and tunnels for underground trains. At the front of the machine, a giant cutting blade spins several times a minute, scouring away rocks and soil that are thrown behind the machine and shuttled away. A machine like this can dig 75 m (250 ft) of tunnel a day.

Sewage pipes use the power of gravity to make waste flow away.

Underground transport systems are fed with air through a complex system of ventilation pipes that link to the surface.

Escalator converts electrical energy into the energy of movement.

Waste heat is generated by trains compressing the air in the tunnels like a bicycle pump.

Electrical rail, hidden between the tracks, powers the train with electrical energy.

The deepest water pipes in New York City are 300 m (1,000 ft) below the ground.

Pipes in the future, will have to be laid even deeper underground, where there is still space to install more pipes.

The future

Fossil fuels were made millions of years in the past and provide 80 per cent of our energy in the present. But that must change in the future as they are causing a problem called global warming, which is changing our planet. Using fossil fuels pollutes cities and increases world tensions, because some countries have less fossil fuels than others. By 2025, it is estimated that industrialized nations will use a third more energy than they do currently, and developing countries, twice as much. To avoid an "energy crisis", we need to realize that energy is one of the most precious things in our world – and use it more wisely.

Wind cowls save energy by using outgoing, stale air to warm incoming, fresh air.

Earth's atmosphere traps some of the Sun's heat.

Heat from the Sun warms Earth.

Sun

Some heat escapes from Earth.

Global warming
Gases in Earth's atmosphere, including carbon dioxide and methane, trap the Sun's heat, warming our planet like a greenhouse. Burning fossil fuels gives off carbon dioxide, causing it to build up in the atmosphere and increase the "greenhouse effect", making the planet hotter. This is called global warming and will have a dramatic impact on Earth's weather, causing climate change.

Energy-saving homes

BedZED (the Beddington Zero-Energy Development) in London is a development of energy-saving homes and offices. Each home and office makes its own energy with solar panels, and was built with local and recycled materials to save energy during construction. There is also a small biopower plant, which burns wood chips.

Large areas of glass trap warmth from the Sun and reduce the need to use central heating.

Outside walls have 30 cm (12 in) of insulation to reduce heat loss.

Carbon-neutral buildings

This factory in Freiburg, Germany, makes 25 per cent of its power using large solar panels, and the rest from a rapeseed-oil biopower plant. Since all its energy comes from renewable sources, its carbon dioxide intake and emissions are balanced, so it does not add to global warming. Buildings like this are described as "carbon neutral".

Local power

Remote power stations supply most of our electricity, two thirds of which is wasted travelling the distance to reach us. The solution to this is "micro-power", with each building making some of its own energy with small wind turbines like these, solar panels, or biopower plants.

Solar-powered car

Sunraycer, a futuristic solar car, won a race travelling 3,140 km (1,950 miles) at speeds up to 113 km/h (70 mph). It makes all of its own energy from solar panels attached to its body. These charge batteries inside the car to power an electric motor that drives the wheels.

WORLD SOLAR CHALLENGE
J. WARD PHILLIPS
16
MICHEL

Facts and figures

There are more than 500 million cars on Earth – one for every 13 people. By 2040, there will be twice as many.

Australia is the world's leading exporter of coal.

A bus emits 10 times less carbon dioxide than a car on a short journey.

Transportation uses more than 50 per cent of the world's oil.

The Middle East supplies almost a third of the world's oil. More oil comes from Saudi Arabia than from any other country.

Wind power is the world's fastest-growing source of energy.

Each electricity generator in the Hoover Dam weighs more than four fully loaded jumbo jets.

An energy-saving light bulb lasts 10 times longer than an ordinary one and uses one fifth as much energy.

China's population is four times bigger than the USA's, but China uses less than half the energy.

There is so much heat trapped inside the Earth that temperatures in the core can reach 7,000°C (12,600°F).

People in Africa and Asia use more than three quarters of the world's wood fuel. More than half of it is used for cooking or home heating.

Canada has a plentiful geothermal potential but, as yet, none has been utilized.

Recycling an aluminium drinks can saves enough energy to power a television for three hours.

The Space Shuttle's main engine makes four times more energy than the Hoover Dam's hydroelectric plant.

People who live in Manhattan, New York, can have their homes heated by steam that flows up from underground pipes.

One basketful of imported food creates more carbon dioxide on its journey than an average family's cooking creates over six months.

Nuclear power stations are so controversial that it can take more than 10 years to plan, design, and build one.

Old Faithful geyser in Yellowstone National Park can release 32,000 litres (8,400 gal) of water in a single eruption, lasting up to 4.5 minutes.

Some estimates suggest that about 40,000 people worldwide may eventually die from the pollution produced by the Chernobyl nuclear explosion of 1986.

In 1879, Thomas Edison – the pioneer of electricity – said, "We will make electricity so cheap that only the rich will burn candles."

There is enough concrete in the Hoover Dam to build a pavement 1.2 m (4 ft) wide around Earth at the Equator.

You could fit 200 trillion uranium atoms on the head of a pin.

You can make electricity by incinerating rubbish, but you need to burn four times more rubbish than coal to release the same amount of energy.

Denmark burns more than half its waste to make electricity, which is more than any other country.

Although fossil fuels are running out, they are expected to provide 90 per cent of world energy by 2020, compared to 70–80 per cent today.

In 1903, Thomas Edison electrocuted an elephant called Topsy with a rival's electricity generating system to prove that it was more dangerous than his own.

Up to 70 million barrels of oil are pumped from the ground each day.

The USA has more coal reserves than any other country. Some of its coal mines are more than 300 m (1,000 ft) deep.

Switching off a computer screen overnight saves enough energy to print 800 pieces of paper.

One in four people worldwide has no access to electricity.

Oil is currently the world's favourite fuel, supplying around 35 per cent of our energy. Coal comes next at 24 per cent and gas is third at 21 per cent.

If world energy use continues to grow at its current rate, global energy consumption will double by 2035 and triple by 2055.

France makes 78 per cent of its energy with nuclear power – more than any other country – but the USA has the most nuclear power plants – 103 of them.

The world's biggest solar power station at Espenhain, Germany, has 33,500 solar panels and makes enough electricity to supply 1,800 homes.

The USA produces more than a third of the world's geothermal power – more than any other country.

Timeline

Energy makes many journeys through the world around us – but our efforts to harness its power have also followed a long journey through time. From the day the Sun started shining billions of years ago to the creation of huge new power stations in the 21st century, people have found increasingly sophisticated ways to make energy work for them.

4–5 billion years ago
The Sun starts shining.

1–2 million years ago
Humans discover fire.

10 million–3000 BCE
People invent more and more tools to make jobs easier (and use the body's energy more efficiently).

3500 BCE
Invention of the wheel in Mesopotamia (now Iraq).

c. 600 BCE
Discovery of static electricity by Greek philosopher Thales of Miletus.

27 CE
Water wheel invented by Roman engineer Vitruvius.

62 CE
Greek scientist Hero of Alexandria invents steam power.

c. 100
Romans first use coal as fuel.

c. 600
Invention of windmills in the Middle East.

c. 1700
Englishmen Thomas Savery and Thomas Newcomen develop the steam engine.

1700s
Christiaan Huygens of Holland conceives the internal combustion engine, but doesn't actually build one.

1800
Italian scientist Alessandro Volta invents the battery (or "Voltaic pile", as it was initially known).

1821
Englishman Michael Faraday invents a crude electric motor.

1830s
William Sturgeon of England develops the first working electric motor.

1831
Michael Faraday demonstrates the principle behind the modern-day electric generator.

1843–1847
English scientist James Prescott Joule explains the conservation of energy theory.

1849
British-born engineer James Francis invents a type of water turbine, now used in most hydroelectric plants.

1859
First oil well drilled in Pennsylvania, USA.

1860s
Étienne Lenoir of Belgium invents the internal combustion engine, and Nikolaus Otto of Germany builds the first working engine.

1870s
German engineers Karl Benz and Gottlieb Daimler develop the first automobiles.

1870s
American Lester Pelton invents a new, more efficient type of hydroelectric turbine (Pelton wheel) to make power for the Californian gold rush.

1879
Thomas Edison of the USA and Joseph Swan of England invent rival electric lights.

1881
Experimental hydroelectric power plant opens in Godalming, England.

1882
Thomas Edison opens the world's first large-scale, commercial power plant in Pearl Street, New York, USA.

1884
Irish engineer Charles Parsons invents the steam turbine (used in virtually every power station).

1885
The first petrol-engine motor car is built by Karl Benz.

1890s
Rudolf Diesel of Germany invents the diesel engine that can run on anything from low-grade petroleum ("diesel") to waste cooking oil and peanuts.

1901
Invention of the first powered vacuum cleaner by British inventor Herbert Booth.

1904
American engineer Herbert Johnson invents the electrically powered food mixer.

1905
German-born physicist Albert Einstein comes up with the basic theory that energy and mass are the same thing ($E=mc^2$), which later inspires the development of nuclear power.

1907
Invention of the electric washing machine by US engineer Alva Fisher.

1912
Josephine Cochran invents the electric dishwasher in the USA.

1928
Invention of the modern-style electric refrigerator.

1942
Construction of the Grand Coulee dam (the USA's biggest hydroelectric dam) is completed.

1942
Italian Enrico Fermi demonstrates the nuclear chain reaction – at the heart of nuclear power plants and bombs.

1948
Hungarian-born scientist Maria Telkes builds the world's first solar-heated house in Massachusetts, USA.

1954
The first nuclear power station is opened in Obinsk, Russia.

1956
The world's first experimental commercial nuclear power plant built at Calder Hall (now Sellafield), England.

1969
The first solar power station is built at Odeillo, France, to provide energy for science experiments.

1973
The world experiences its first major energy crisis in the aftermath of the Yom Kippur War in the Middle East.

1982
Construction of the world's largest hydroelectric dam (Itaipu, in Brazil/Paraguay) completed.

1986
One of the reactors at a nuclear power station at Chernobyl in the Ukraine explodes.

2004
The world's biggest solar power station opens in Espenhain, Germany.

2008
China's Yangtze dam becomes the world's largest hydroelectric plant when construction is finally completed.

Glossary

Absolute zero
The lowest theoretically possible temperature (-273.15°C or -459.67°F). At absolute zero, atoms and molecules have zero kinetic energy.

Air resistance
The force of the air that pushes against moving objects, causing them to lose kinetic energy.

Atom
The smallest part of a chemical element that can exist. An atom is made from a central nucleus with electrons orbiting around it.

Bacterium (plural bacteria)
A single-celled, microscopic organism that lives in huge numbers in all available habitats, such as in soil, water, and the human body.

Big Bang
The explosion that is believed to have started the Universe about 13.7 billion years ago.

Biodiesel
A type of fuel, made from materials such as soya beans or recycled vegetable oils, that can be burned in a diesel engine.

Biomass
Plants, such as straw and willow trees, that are grown deliberately to be used as fuel.

Calorie
A measurement of how much energy something contains, often used to compare foods. A calorie (which is short for kilocalorie) is equal to 4.185 Joules of energy.

Carbon dioxide
The gas that is produced when fuels containing hydrogen and carbon burn in the air. Carbon dioxide builds up in the atmosphere, contributing to climate change.

Climate change
The change to Earth's weather patterns, including a gradual warming of temperature, caused by burning fossil fuels.

Combustion
A chemical reaction in which a fuel burns with oxygen to produce carbon dioxide and water, giving off heat energy.

Conduction
The way in which heat energy passes directly between two objects that are touching.

Conservation of energy
The theory that energy can never be created or destroyed, only converted into different forms.

Convection
The way in which heat energy swirls gradually through a gas or liquid.

Cooling tower
A chimney attached to a power station that cools water for reuse.

Crust
The rocks that make up Earth's outer surface.

Current electricity
A type of electricity that carries electrical energy around a closed path or circuit.

Cylinder
A strong metal container inside an engine where fuel burns to release energy.

Derrick
The tower from which an oil rig's drill is suspended.

Efficiency
A measurement of how much energy something uses well and how much it wastes. An engine that is 40 per cent efficient uses only 40 per cent of the energy from its fuel and wastes the rest.

Electricity
A form of energy involving charged particles, either as a current or stored statically.

Electron
A tiny particle that can carry electrical energy through cables and wires, and causes magnetism.

Emissions
The waste gases that are released when fuels are burned. Carbon dioxide emissions are one of the causes of global warming.

Engine
A machine that burns fuel to release heat energy and provide mechanical power.

Entropy
The idea that all energy travels in the same direction – from order to chaos, and never the other way. All energy ends up as chaotic waste heat.

Ethanol
A type of alcohol that can be produced from plants and used to power diesel engines.

Explosion
A rapid release of energy that generates a large, expanding volume of gas, moving at very high speeds.

Fibre optics
The use of thin glass fibres to transmit light signals. The light travels along the fibres in straight lines.

Force
A pushing or pulling action that can change an object's shape or the way it moves.

Fossil fuel
A fuel, such as oil, gas, or coal, that is formed over millions of years from the remains of plants and animals.

Friction
The rubbing force between two objects that are in contact. The friction between a car tyre and the road causes the car to lose kinetic energy and slow down.

Fuel
Material burnt as a source of energy to provide heat, power machines, or produce a nuclear reaction.

Gasohol
A mixture of ethanol and petrol used as a fuel to power motor vehicles.

Generator
A machine packed with coils of wire and magnets that spin around and generate electricity.

Geothermal
A type of heat energy made by hot rocks inside Earth's crust and mantle.

Geyser
A spout of hot water and steam that emerges from weak points in Earth's surface, and is powered by the planet's geothermal energy.

Global warming
The gradual warming of Earth's atmosphere and oceans. Global warming happens because of a build up of carbon dioxide in the upper atmosphere, caused by burning fossil fuels.

Glucose
A type of sugar used to store and transport energy inside animals and plants.

Heat
Energy stored by atoms and molecules vibrating inside an object.

Heat death
A theory that suggests that the Universe will eventually run out of useful energy, like a battery gradually running flat.

Hydroelectricity
A method of making electricity by channelling water from a river through a turbine to power a generator.

Insulation
A material that surrounds an object to reduce the heat energy that can flow into or out of it.

Joule
A measurement of energy. A kilojoule is 1,000 Joules and a megajoule is one million Joules.

Kinetic energy
The energy something has because it is moving or converting stored potential energy into another form.

Magma
The molten rock inside Earth's crust and mantle.

Mantle
The thick layer of molten rock in between Earth's crust (outer rock) and core (inner rock).

Matter
A physical substance that has mass and occupies space.

Methane
A gas made from carbon and hydrogen that can be burned as fuel.

Molecule
A collection of two or more atoms joined together to make a substance.

Motor
A machine that converts energy into movement. Most motors generate a spinning motion that can power another machine.

Nuclear fission
A process that makes energy by splitting the centre (nucleus) of a large atom.

Nuclear fusion
A process that makes energy by joining together two or more small atoms (or fragments of atoms).

Nucleus
The central part of an atom, made up of smaller particles called protons and neutrons.

PET scan
Positron Emission Tomography (PET) involves injecting a radioactive substance into a patient. This substance is picked up by a scanner to create a three-dimensional picture of part of the human body.

Photosynthesis
A chemical reaction inside plants that uses sunlight to turn water and carbon dioxide into food.

Photovoltaic
A type of solar panel that makes electricity from sunlight.

Piston
A plunger that moves inside a cylinder, converting heat energy into mechanical energy to power a machine.

Potential energy
The energy stored by an object, which can be used later.

Radiation
A type of electromagnetic energy that objects such as the Sun give off. The Sun's radiant energy is a mixture of light and heat.

Renewable
A source of energy that will not run out, but will be replaced.

Resistance
The opposition to an electric current in a circuit, which results in some of the energy being lost as waste heat.

Solar energy
The energy that comes from the Sun.

Spark plug
The part of an internal combustion engine that produces the spark to ignite the fuel mixture.

Static electricity
A type of electricity that builds up in one place, such as the electricity in a thundercloud.

Substation
A small electricity plant that converts the high-voltage energy from a power station into lower-voltage power for homes and offices.

Temperature
A measurement of how hot or cold something is.

Thermal energy
Another way of describing heat energy.

Turbine
A machine that spins around when a gas or liquid passes through it. Windmills, wind turbines, and water turbines are examples. A turbine can drive a generator to make electricity.

Ultraviolet
A type of electromagnetic radiation found in sunlight.

Uranium
A heavy, radioactive element used as the fuel for nuclear power stations.

Volcano
An open channel in Earth's crust that allows molten rock (lava) to pour out during an eruption.

Waste heat
The energy wasted when something does not work efficiently. Car engines, power stations, and the human body all waste some of the fuel they consume as waste heat.

Water cycle
The circulation of water between Earth's surface and its atmosphere.

Watt
A measurement of how quickly something uses energy. One watt is equal to using one Joule each second. A 100-watt lamp uses 100 J of energy every second.

Wind chill
The way temperature feels cooler because the wind is blowing and removing heat energy.

Yellowcake
A type of concentrated uranium powder made during the production of nuclear fuel.

Index

Credits

The publisher would like to thank the following for their kind permission to reproduce their photographs:

Abbreviations: a=above; b=below/bottom; c=centre; f=far; l=left; r=right; t=top.

2 **DK Images**: Alistair Duncan. 4 **Getty Images**: Photographer's Choice / Gary S Chapman (bl). 4-5 **DK Images**: Russell Sadur (c). 5 **Alamy Images**: Kos Picture Source (cr). **DK Images**: Frank Greenaway (bc). **Rex Features**: Chris Balcombe (tc). 6 **DK Images**: Brian Cosgrove (c). 6-7 **Getty Images**: Photographer's Choice / John Lawrence (b). 7 **Alamy Images**: blickwinkel (bl); Jeff Morgan (tc). **DK Images**: Andy Crawford / Peter Minister (cr). Getty Images: Altrendo Images (bc). 8 **DK Images**: Andy Crawford / Peter Minister (tl). 8-9 **Corbis**: Kevin Fleming (c). 9 **Alamy Images**: A T Willett (tc). **Corbis**: John D Norman (cra); Sygma / Patrick Robert (bc). **DK Images**: (c). 10 **Alamy Images**: David Taylor (c). **Corbis**: Reuters / Claor Cortes IV (cr). 11 **Corbis**: Christopher Morris (fcl); Paul A Souders (cl). **DK Images**: Demetrio Carrasco (cr). **Getty Images**: Image Bank / Grant Faint (bc). **NASA**: (fcr). **Science Photo Library**: Ian Hooton (bl). 12 **Alamy Images**: Steven May (bc); Janusz Wrobel (clb). **Corbis**: Michael Prince (tl). 12-13 **Corbis**: David Arky (c). 13 **Alamy Images**: Jon Arnold Images (r); Pacific Press Servce (tc). **Corbis**: Zefa / Dietrich Rose (c). 14 **DK Images**: Clive Streeter (br). 15 **DK Images**. 16 **NASA**: 2004-34-b (br). 17 **Alamy Images**: David Hoffman Photo Library (tr). **Corbis**: Paul C Chauncey (tc). **Getty Images**: Romilly Lockyer (tl). 18 **Alamy Images**: Mark Sykes (bl). **Corbis**: John Brecher (cl). **DK Images**: Andreas Einsiedel (bc/peat) (bc/coal) (bc/anthracite); Emma Firth (tl); Courtesy of the Natural History Museum, London / Colin Keates (bc/lignite) (bc/plant matter). 18-19 **Getty Images**: Stone / Keith Wood (c). 19 **DK Images**: Steve Gorton (cr); David Peart (cl). 20 **Alamy Images**: Transtock Inc. (c). **DK Images**: Linda Whitwam (bc). 20-21 **NASA**: (c). 21 **DK Images**: (bl); Rob Reichenfeld (tc). **Rex Features**: Phil Rees (cr). 22 **DK Images**: (c). 22-23 **DK Images**: Gerard Brown (c). 23 **DK Images**: Jerry Young (bc). 24 **Alamy Images**: The Photolibrary Wales (br). **Science Photo Library**: Edward Kinsman (l). 25 **Corbis**: Schlegelmilch (br). **DK Images**: Christopher & Sally Gable (cl); Chris Stowers (tr). 26 **DK Images**: Steve Shott (cl); Tony Souter (tr); Neil Sutherland (c). 27 **Corbis**: Zefa / Estelle Klawitter (cr). **DK Images**: Alamy / Comstock (c); Trish Gant (tl); Magnus Rew (tc). 28 **DK Images**: M Balan (bl). **Still Pictures**: Fritz Polking (br). 28-29 **DK Images**: Oxford Scientific Films / Tim Shepard (c). 29 **Alamy Images**: Rick & Nora Bowers (cr). **DK Images**: Andy Crawford (br); Francesca Yorke (tr). 30 **NASA**: EIT Consortium (ESA/NASA) (bl). 31 **DK Images**: NASA (tr). **NASA**: ESA (br); JPL / SOHO (c). 36 **Corbis**: (r); Australian Picture Library / John Carnemolla (c). **DK Images**: Courtesy of The Science Museum, London / Clive Streeter (clb). **Science Photo Library**: US Department of Energy (bl). 37 **Photograph Courtesy of EFDA-JET**: (bl). **Science Photo Library**: Lawrence Livermore Laboratory (cl); Hank Morgan (cr). 38 **DK Images**: Demetrio Carrasco (cl). **Science Photo Library**: David Nunuk (br). 39 **Corbis**: Owaki - Kulla (t). DK Images: Sean Hunter (bl); Chris Stowers (br). 41 **Alamy Images**: Tim Graham (r). **DK Images**: Andy Holligan (cl); James Stevenson (cb). **Getty Images**: Carsten Peter (tl). **Michael Reinhardt**: (bl). 42 **DK Images**: Dave King (b). 43 **DK Images**: Nigel Hicks (tl); Rough Guides / Greg Ward (tr). **http://sl.wikipedia.org**: (bl). 44 **Getty Images**: Stone / Tony Page (bl); Taxi / Peter Adams (c). 44-45 **DK Images**: Demetrio Carrasco (c). 45 **DK Images**: Peter Anderson (bl); Philip Dowell (cr); Dave King (tr). Getty Images: Mark Wilson (br). **Science Photo Library: US Department of Energy / NREL** (cl). 46 **DK Images**: Mike Dunning (c). 46-47 **Still Pictures**: Oed (c). 47 **Corbis**: Zefa / Joson (br). **DK Images**: Andy Crawford (c); Nigel Hicks (tc). Getty Images: Stone+ / Tara Moore (tl). 49 **Alamy Images**: Eryrie (tl). **Still Pictures**: Gene Rhoden (tr). 50 **Getty Images**: America 24-7 / Bobby Model (br); Image Bank / Paul McCormick (cl). 51 **Mads Eskesen**: (tr). **Getty Images**: AFP Photo / Liu Jin (bc). 52 **Alamy Images**: Andrew Holt (tc); Geraint Lewis (l). 53 **Alamy Images**: qaphotos.com (tc). **Getty Images**: Dennis O'Clair (tl). 54 **DK Images**: NASA (cl). 54-55 **Alamy Images**: View Pictures Ltd (c). 55 **Alamy Images**: Clynt Garnham (cr). **DK Images**: Courtesy of Phil Farrand / Dave King (br). **Science Photo Library**: Martin Bond (tc)

Jacket images:
Front: Science Photo Library: Alfred Pasieka (b). **Back: Alamy Images**: Ace Stock Limited (cr); Kos Picture Source (br); **DK Images**: Gerard Brown (clb). **Getty Images**: Image Bank / Eric Meola (bl); **Science Photo Library**: Alfred Pasieka (Background); **Still Pictures**: Kent Wood (cla). **Back Flap: DK Images**: Frank Greenaway

All other images © Dorling Kindersley
For further information see: **www.dkimages.com**

Dorling Kindersley would also like to thank:
Hazel Beynon for proofreading; Lynn Bresler for the index; Hoa Luc for editorial assistance; and Marilou Prokopiou for additional artworks.